Praise for Despojo

What Tatiana has done with *Despojo* is pure delight! She offers home, love, peace and healing. Her heritage woven into each line, sharing her roots and the wisdom from her ancestors. With each poem, she tells a story with a quiet yet bold flare that only she possesses. Masterfully written and a complete gem is this masterpiece!

—C. Thomas, Poet & Author of *Bernard's Bedroom*

Despojo waters us with a conversation of identity Caribeños know all too well. A refreshing exploration of both wanting to belong and tracing back all that makes us feel seen. This collection reminds us that it is in the shedding of skin that we learn to mend.

—Melania-Luisa Marte, Poet & Author of *Mela*

Despojo is a testament to so many things: the pain and healing in the aftermath of sexual violence, the lineages Tatiana honors and writes within, the fact that love is a verb. The poems in *Despojo* carry an impossible amount of compassion for their subjects. I learn from Tatiana Figueroa Ramirez the act of staying put and just looking; she is a poet deeply invested in witnessing her family and ancestry, in writing with an uncompromising eye towards balancing the truth and the turmoil. She never turns away. I am so lulled by her language, which is so skillful it has a spine. Flowers dot the pages, the air becomes thinner and sweet with molasses. Do yourself a favour and learn what it really means to trace lineage, to write with strength towards people who have hurt you, to stand and carry an entire history on your shoulders.

—Nancy Huang, Author of *Favorite Daughter*

DESPOJO

Poems by
Tatiana Figueroa Ramírez

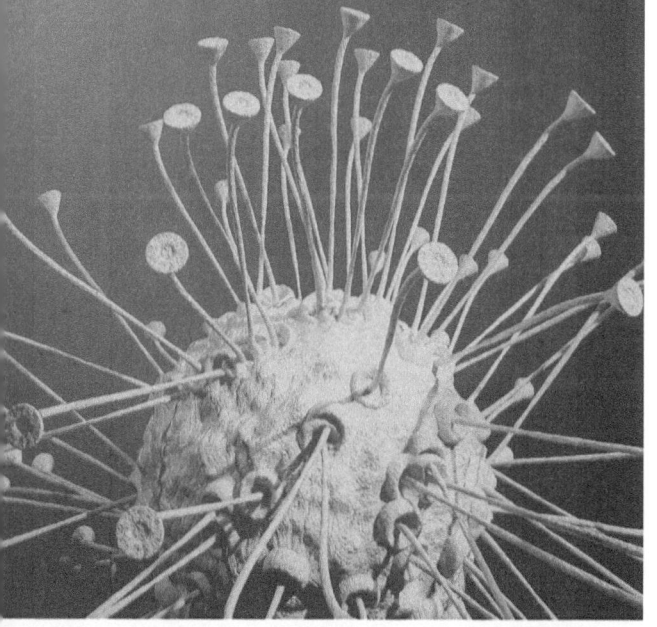

FlowerSong Books
McAllen, Texas 78501
Copyright © 2020 by Tatiana Figueroa Ramírez

ISBN: 978-1-7345617-2-2

Published by FlowerSong Books
in the United States of America.
www.flowersongbooks.com

Set in Adobe Garamond Pro

Cover design and typeset by Matthew Revert
Author photograph by Jazmin Samora

No part of this book may be reproduced without written permission from the publisher.

All inquiries and permission requests should be addressed to the Publisher.

These poems are for the ones who need a cleansing, a stripping, a removal, un despojo of the vibrations holding them back from living in their true light.

Table of Contents

9	Despojo
11	Mi Niña Pequeña
13	Daddy's Little Girl
15	Calladita Te Ves Más Bonita
18	La Negra
22	I Do, But I Don't
28	Pro Choice
31	To Abuelo Papo
33	I Went to You Last Night
35	A Poem that Remembers
39	Spring's Rebirth Haikus
40	Black Boy
42	Passe Blanc
44	Reunions in Baltimore
46	Bomba
48	Perfumes
51	Acknowledgements

Despojo

Your chest heavy, absorbing
molasses air. Hands tremble.
This energy is not yours.
Anger & tears flood
your body. Category 5 inundated
streetveins & rivers, so you pray
to María.

Despójate.

Let water blessed
by the virgin herself drench
you. Frigid. Inhale
cigar smoke fresh from La Habana. Feel
heat from blue orange flames at your feet.
Santa Barbara's gala apple skin scarf cloaks
you. Chant verses learned in church harmonize
with bronze bells ringing
around you. Rose water fills
atmosphere with morning dew light.

Despójate.

Imagine clouded demons pushed
away & howling screams forgotten. Scrape
pain from your body & wash
sadness off of your sternum.
Vibrations tremor to disappear. Cast
this all far from you with intent. Deny
permission for anything to return.
Throw it to the fire.   Changó.
Throw it to the water.   Ochún.
Throw it to the heavens.   Obatalá.

Despójate.

Mi Niña Pequeña

"Mi niña pequeña.
What happened to her?" asks
a mother. She kisses
her daughter's forehead.
Hands linger
on a rosey cheek.
It recoils
into a cold blanket.

The girl recalls
a mother chatting
with her favorite tías.
Café Bustelo in oversized mugs.
The topic: How a mother planned
to kill
herself. The rope remains
in the basement. She brags.

Her daughter hears
the extended album of shoes crashing
into walls, dents birthed

onto stainless steel trash cans, & kicks banging
broken down bathroom doors. It plays
in an endless loop.

Her daughter remembers
melodies of sibling threats
of running away mixed
with a mother chorusing
"You'll miss me when I'm gone."
Songs stuck on play.

Her daughter's tears pound
against a lavenderlaced pillowcase.
The sound is too loud.
Headaches wish
her daughter a good morning.
Sharp pains kiss
her daughter goodnight.

What happened to her daughter?
"I'm just tired," cries
a mother's niña pequeña.

Daddy's Little Girl

My creator & king
since conception.

I once saw   distance
when thinking   *Father.*

Fears of a disappearing
dad   heightened.
Temptation to cheat
victorious.
High price of   separation.

Teen self searched
for him   in his one bedroom apartment.
Teen self cried
for him   in the movies we watched.
Teen self waited
for him   during the errands we ran.
Teen self needed
for him   to hold her & not walk away.
Teen self begged
for him   to stay.

I wanted my daddy.
As wrong as he was.

Teen self reached
for him & his hands.
We moved
closer together
connected & confused
as to what should come
next, yet
a bond birthed
& smiles survived.

I remember
the distance that was
my father. & I still want
my daddy in my life.

Calladita Te Ves Más Bonita

The leather beneath sends
chills to my pores. Legs hang
lifeless. No movement is said
to make this
painless.
The nurse's hand wrapped
in latex grips
my forearm. A rubber band cuts
off circulation.

I look up to Mami,
                she said

                        "They don't like it when
                        little girls complain."

She watches
silently.

The halogen lights take me to the mall. It is
winter & the evening is dark.
A South Asian woman cleans
her kiosk & a man shares
all he will do to her after hours.

She says
nothing
& keeps covering the oils adorned
with cute bows, not bending
over too much. I stand
mango lemonade in hand
silent.

A needle pierces
numb skin searching
for blood. Transparent tubes turn
scarlet. My arm,
a watercolor painting, blends
shades of tan & white to
hues of blue.

Dull colors carry
me under a tree canopy.
The cluster of evergreens beyond
my backyard. The one past the playground.
An autumn sun pokes
behind the silhouette of a
friend. She on top.
She unbuttoning.
Me still.
Me silent.

The rubber is
rough & tight, squeezing
Ow through my lips.
Mami & nurse flash
their eyes at me.
Mami's glare repeats
her words & my mouth seals
shut.

Eyes closed.
It is black & I feel
him pressed against me.
Each thrust a reminder.
I did say no.
I repeatedly said no
before I laid.
Silent.

The nurse smiles.
I'm released.
"What a good girl,"
She says.

I smile.
Silent.

La Negra

"You're Scary Spice,"
says the golden haired girl.
The one labeled Scary
stays silent.
A third little girl
strings her words
to win the role
of Baby Spice
and the golden girl
becomes Ginger.
The three play
singing and dancing
just to repeat it all
the next day.

20 years pass,
the one labeled Scary
stares back at me.
Her honey toned coils
highlight her face
and complement
her sand-freckled

hands & feet.
Her light brown eyes
scream
I'm surviving the struggle.
The struggle of
raising my badass brother,
working for a fucked up
education system,
and trying to love myself,
all while learning
how to bend my knee & walk again.

The one labeled Scary
is now a free mermaid,
swimming
in a ten feet deep ocean
with the golden haired girl,
who is quickly called away
by her golden haired father.
"My father said I can't play with —"
is all she says.
Salty tears
disappear
into chlorine fused waves
as the one labeled Scary

sinks deeper
drowning her body.
Echoes of Papa saying
"You are not a —"
rip through each ripple.

A scar squats
on her chin's right side,
downward turned lips
carry the weight of loss,
and a Deathly Hallows tattoo
attempts to protect her
from the curse of being a –.

The Bronx,
The Boogie Down
full of boogeymen
is the one labeled Scary's
home again,
where the Nuyorican,
street culture
shapes her,
but the images of
Mami and Abuela
challenge her.

They are light
like the color of coquito.
Their hair doesn't need any heat.
If they are Puerto Rican,
then she is the negra of the block.

The moonlight pours down.
She oozes with magic
as her hair defies gravity.
Cheeks are soft.
No hard edges.
Her gaze tender
and present.
The one labeled Scary
is not Scary.
The one labeled Scary
is not a –.

Negra, you are Puerto Rican.

I Do, But I Don't

You say
you love me,
I don't believe you.
"Más vale
que no tengas novia."
"No, no.
I'm not like that,"
you said
in Spanish dressed English.
We laughed it off.

When you say
"Me quiero casar contigo,"
translation
"I want my green card."
You tell me I'm perfect,
the perfect opportunity
for a come up.
What's App notifications,
incoming calls
are daily. Your mother
echándome la bendición

is ritual. Confirmation
emails from JetBlue arrive
unexpectedly.
All existing love songs
not enough,
so you make them up.

I still don't believe you.

Twelve years ago, I begged
my father not to leave.
We sat
on the living room floor
of our empty house.
His eyes
never looked up.
I'm sure
he could describe
every fiber of that cheap,
camelskinned carpet.
I begged.
       He tried getting up.
I begged.
       He almost walked out.
I begged.

He said
"I need to choose
my happiness."
I stopped begging.

My grandfathers were
loyal men to those they loved.
Abuelo Papo.
Never cheated
unlike the countless
mujeriegos in the family tree.
Received
communion every Sunday.
Had a favorite son
who was not my father.
Had favorite grandchildren
who were not
me or mine.
      Only called his favorites.
      Only cared for his favorites.
      Only knew his favorites.
Abuelo Tongo's life
with his first wife,
my grandmother, came
before his loyal days.

       He did not know my name.
       He did not know my age.
       He did not know loyalty
to me & mine.
However, he had memorized
each piece of the children lacking
his blood. He loved
their kids & never missed
a birthday.
"Tío Tongo" once leaked
from my lips & a quick fix of
"Abuelo" relaxed
his eyes.

Tío Mickey killed
himself when I was 12.
Tío Edwin in & out
of jail until he died, too.
My favorite cousin went
away.
Papito.
The best I had.
My great-grandfather had
trouble controlling his fists & enjoyed
stepping out, but he did love

me & mine,
unconditionally.

& now there's you.

I landed
in Santo Domingo, you held
three roses & a heart shaped balloon.
Your dimpled smile pushed
through the crowd. You wore
"My heart is yours
my Dolly" on your white tee.
I left
Santo Domingo, you cried.
Hugged me tightly & said
"I love you."

Now, I sit
on grass-ridden,
stone steps
somewhere
in the states.
My phone lights up.
Another notification.
It reads

"Te amo mi pushita."
I smile.
The floral, setting sun
becomes
more vibrant,
& I leave
the message on read.

Pro Choice

      "I'm pregnant."
My mother's hand clenches
her wicker chair.
Fingernails scratch
my name from her will.
Her stare cuts
into my womb, trying to verify
my truth.
Her mouth quietly loads
the rounds for my execution.

By my age,
she was married
& mother of two.
I was supposed to be different.
Her chair's creaking cries
      "Lord knows,
the island doesn't need
another single mother.
A God send for the government.
A reason to reinstate sterilization."
& here I am.

19 & pregnant.
No degree in hand.
No ring on my finger.

  "You'll go to New York
& get rid of it."
Her words freeze
the flaming blossoms
of the flamboyant tree
in our yard.
  "You'll go to New York
& give it away."
The ice extends down
to the once evergreen grass
outside our home.
  "Mami!"

Her brow twitches count
the choices I have.

One.
Be a marine biologist.
Two.
Be a decent wife.
Three.

Be pure again.
Four.
No one would have to know.

My throat burns
from the steaming syllables I swallow.
My veins burst
pushing back the pressure.
My knees buckle
attempting to control
the collapsing ideas in my head.

A tear counts
the choices given.
One.
Don't dare
be a mother.

To Abuelo Papo

Your light eyes pierce through oversized glasses, peering over a sangria colored couch. You stare straight at me. My arrival, to you, in another language. I catch a glimpse of your milky hair. Straight strands so short attentive ears poke out on each side of your head. Their wingspan as wide as your frame.

Once-broad shoulders now hunch into your chest. You look small like the folded piece of paper in my pocket. I search your body for the Army veteran from pictures. The man who stood tall in olive & café con leche tinted fatigues. I can't see him past the skindressed skeleton on view in my living room. I can't tell how much life runs through those bones.

Your eyes & mine lock again. I give you a hug. Careful not to spill over your vegetable soup. Careful not to knock over your cane. Careful not to hold you too close. I don't feel the weight of your legs by my side. The same legs that walked you to la panadería & back. I don't feel heat from your shrunken arms. Your *José* tattoo is illegible.

The elderly, moss ink now looking like a birthmark above your elbow.

You once said I could hold down a house in a hurricane. You once joked I was infected with fungus. You, never within reach. You who once was a grandfather I hated seeing, yet here you are right next to me, renaming me Preciosa & Princesa. You tell me you love me. You repeat you're happy to see me again. I believe you.

I tell you I love you, too, trying to forget the tumors thriving inside you. I say I'm glad you visited as my fingertips clutch your knuckles. I make sure you hear me each time.

I Went to You Last Night

Tears tied knots in my throat & I grabbed
your face. One hand cupping
each shriveled cheek. I took
in every line you inherited
from 87 years you made
seem effortless. My fingers felt
the cancer that consumed
Tío Chucho, your son. They heard
the gunshot that killed
Tío Mickey, your nieto. They saw
the operation that stole
fertility, your legacy.

Your body still.
I spoke
& you silent.
Your eyes barren
as the quenepa trees in winter.
Your muted stare slashed
through me to the corner of the room.
There was nothing. You said
"Es la novia de Junior."

    No.
I was not my brother's girlfriend.

Streams from gentle sea ripples rolled
down my face as defeated lips kissed
your wrinkles. My eyes looked
into yours once more & pupils connected.
Vision misty & blurred. I repeated
    I love you.
    I love you.
    I love you so much.
I hoped you would learn
the words, but you never did.

A Poem that Remembers

There's a poem. She floats
in the air afraid of being.
She hides
behind errands & thoughts sent
to the back of my mind. She whispers
        "I remember
        the club was loud & hot. It was July.
        Ice melted
        under amber rum.
        Refill after refill, his eyes narrowed.
        Glassy. His body pulled
        away. He tossed
        your purse to the side.
        You said he was drunk.
        He called you selfish, but
        he doesn't remember.
        He doesn't remember saying
        you thought you were better.
        He doesn't remember saying
        you were cold.
        He doesn't remember saying
        you didn't love him."

The poem sits
in front of me. Her voice clear
as my own.
> "He doesn't remember
> how you gave him water.
> He doesn't remember
> how you helped him into bed.
> He doesn't remember
> how quiet the room was
> until - you - against a wall yelled

Stop it!
Stop it!
Stop!

> He doesn't remember
> pushing you.
> He doesn't remember
> being on top of you..."

The poem nears
the page nervous to feel
wet ink flow
through her form. She shivers
from its chill. She knows

she'll no longer be
a bodiless memory
> "I remember
> you crying.
> Your face bloodshot, burned
> by heated tears.
> Your eyes swollen, overflowing
> with salty streams.
> He never knew it. He laid
> inches from you
> & he never knew it."

The poem knows she is   truth.
> "I remember you walked
> through the gardens. Roses of Sharon still
> moist from last night's thunderstorm, smelling
> like velorios & funeral homes. You wore
> a black dress with white polka dots reflecting
> his speckles of hope. I remember
> he unveiled a ring & forced
> it onto your finger before
> you ever said yes.
>
> I remember you forsook
> the ring on the bedside table, saying

you wanted to talk.
I remember at dinner he said
you promised to say yes.
    I remember
    you never said yes.
    I remember
    you said no.
        I remember
          you said no.
            I remember.

                  You said no. You said no.
                  You said no. You said no.
                  You said no. You said no.
                  You said no. You said no.
                  You said no. You said no.

                  You said no. You said no.
                  You said no. You said no.
                  You said no. You said no.
                  You said no. You said no.
                  You said no. You said no.

                  You said no. You said no.
                  You said no. You said no.
                  You said no. You said no.
                  You said no. You said no.

Spring's Rebirth Haikus

Concrete blooms color
gardens we wish wouldn't die.
Welcome. Please don't leave.

Raindrops to wash us.
Raindrops to see reflections.
Raindrops. More raindrops.

Breezes kiss my hair.
Consent was never given,
But they say it's love.

Black Boy

He was a Black Boy from
the south. Tennessee.
A stint in Alabama.
Ignorance explained.
Bubble living I needed
to burst. My purpose.

He wasn't a racist.

He was a Black Boy raised
   by his Black parents, living
      with his Black grandparents, knowing
         his Black aunts & uncles, playing
            with his Black brothers & sisters.

He was a Black Boy from
the south. Confederate flag
not representing
rebellion to retain
slavery, but southern pride
to those with Lannister lion locs
& wintertime eyes.

He was a Black Boy from
the south. 1 out of every 6 to 8
on the street looking
like him & conservatives have
the only say. Forget
Black Women. Ignore
me.

He told me
"You're drama & I avoid drama."

Drama
   in place of
        Black.
           Blackness.
My Blackness.
His own Blackness.

He was a Black Boy who hated
being   a Black Boy.

Passe Blanc

Curls thrive untamed & shoulder width. Or
no moist air plus an aggressive blow out to train
each strand straight like a ballerina's back.
An easy wet & wavy is what they call
a good hair day.

Wintry skin is coquito, coconut cream & vanilla with
hints of cinnamon & cloves. My summer glow
the love child of a bond with the sun.

English is Maryland adapted, adorned
by traces of New York. No signs of
a fluent Spanish speaker when
the Boricua beast sleeps.

Saturday morning in New Orleans.
Brunch is the move for my two best friends,
their cousin, & myself. Their cocoa skin matches
Herbert's coffee complexion. He our Uber driver.
He dances to Drake. He tells us stories.
He five stars worthy. He nicknames us each.

"You know what we call girls like you around here? Passe blanc."

Mix coquito colored skin with wet & wavy coils
& racial ambiguity allows the option to pass
as something I'm not, camouflage identities
for that of another's, something I do not wish to explore.

Passe blanc.

To benefit from passing
is to deny my name,
is to denounce the mothers
who forged the rivers in my blood vessels,
is to forget the island womb,
is to neglect the struggle
that spelled my bones.

Reunions in Baltimore

We sit.
Wooden fenced backyard highlights
a coal colored fire escape kissing
parched grass. Tired street lamps, hidden stars,
& bug repelling torches keep
our faces bright enough.

We listen.
Acoustic cocktails seep
through a struggling screen door. Sounds slip
past a slurred, political cypher & bounce
on the concrete patio.

Reunited.
Quench our musethirst.
What makes you smile?
  People's passions
    Butterflies
      The sun
Do you remember?
  Walking to the gas station
    Motion Toy

                              Loud as shit

What inspires you?
         Nature
                   Hope
                              Juxtaposition

Mmms & Ooos interject
into conversations.
Laughter lingers
between siren rings
from nearby streets.
The memory of a man loading
a gun two blocks away now repainted.
A story told with light hearted tones.
A story not meant for this moment.

We sit & listen. Reunited.
In peace.

Bomba

Mi respeto al tambor.
Bow my head
to the gods & ancestors

                              living

in the beat of my veins.
Proceed with grace, smooth
over every jagged edge
bare feet feel.

Root into legacy,
    I dust off my path.
        Skirt's hem a broom.
            Dirt floor demons I walk over.
                Sweep & sweep & sweep.
            Space cleansed.
        Circle my ground.
    Pace back & forth.
A lioness in my den.

Buleador fuerte keeps
    the rhythm in my chest rippling
        through my body. Waves hit

        me over & over.
           This isn't over. Spirits bang
     on my sternum & escape
    through my shoulders. Enamorá
  del macho. Cucando
al subidor. El primo fiel
no se aparta de mi ritmo.
I go. He follows.

Tempos quicken.
Hard beats drop.
No se para el piquete.
Folds in my skirt run up & down.
    Como los taínos
        up & down
            the mountains.
                Like los Africanos
        up & down the fields.
    Like our children
up & down the streets.

¡Bomba!

Mi respeto al tambor.

Perfumes

It begins outside. In your backyard or the trees down the road by the basketball court. Usually, in your grandmother's garden.
You'll need
   lavender
      roses
         lilies
           & mums.
           To relax the strain stuck in the base of your neck. To perfume the space around your mind & calm your shiver. To purify open wounds from the permanence of scars. To ease your breath, allowing laughter to wake again.

   Think good thoughts.

It moves inside. In your home or that of a loved one under the veil of God's hand. It will always be in the kitchen.
You'll need

aged rum
    boiling water
        a caldero
            & a vase.
            To preserve the sugar scents dancing through the liquid ripples. To steam clear clogged channels for positive energy. To contain the power brewing over the flame. To display the beauty of oblate blooms & blessed liquids.

Think good thoughts.

It grows deeper. In your heart & in your spirit. In your valves, guiding the blood of ancestors through your body.
You'll need
    memory
        gratitude
            humility
                & purpose.
                To thank the blossoms for their sacrifice & gifts. To invoke protective beings feeding your fragrant caldo.

To set your intentions for creating these waters, birthing a bouquet, & cleansing yourself.

Think good thoughts.

Acknowledgements

Thank you to the publications where the following poems were first published.

"La Negra," *The Acentos Review*, November 2016
"Reunions in Baltimore," *A Gypsy's Library*, September 2017
"Bomba," *Queen Mob's Teahouse*, March 2018
"Despojo," *Coconut Curls y Café con Leche*, August 2019
"Calladita Te Ves Más Bonita," *Coconut Curls y Café con Leche*, August 2019
"Pro Choice," *Coconut Curls y Café con Leche*, August 2019

I must thank my mother for being my spiritual base throughout my life. She is the handful of roses in homemade alcoholado, the scent from burning incense, and the light of a candle wick. Without my mother, I would not believe so much in a good despojo. Without her, I would not be here today.

I also want to thank my grandmothers and loved ones who never stopped praying. They pray for me, our family, our home, our world. Their prayers add to the force of a despojo and, without them, all of this would be for nothing.

Thank you to Edward and the FlowerSong Press familia for believing in these poems and giving them a place. These experiences needed a safe space and that's what they were given.

Thank you to each person who contributed to these poems. To those who gave feedback. To those who listened. To those who shared their stories and allowed me to pass them on.

Lastly, I must thank you for making it here. I appreciate you reading these poems and letting these moments be heard. I acknowledge, at times, these poems can be heavy, but they are always necessary. My hope is that this journey can serve as a piece of the healing process for many of you. My hope is that you will leave these poems renewed. My hope is that you can move forward after this despojo.

Born in Puerto Rico and raised in the mainland United States, Tatiana Figueroa Ramirez graduated with a B.A. in English Literature from the University of Maryland, Baltimore County (UMBC) and is a VONA Voices Alumna, having worked with award winning poets Willie Perdomo and Danez Smith. Tatiana currently performs, teaches poetry workshops, and hosts events in the greater Washington DC area, having previously done so in New York, Philadelphia, Miami, Puerto Rico, and the Dominican Republic at venues including New York University, The Kennedy Center, and The Howard Theatre. You can read her work in *The Acentos Review*, *Here Comes Everyone*, and *Queen Mob's Teahouse*, among other publications. She is also the author of *Coconut Curls y Café con Leche*.

www.ingramcontent.com/pod-product-compliance
Lightning Source LLC
Chambersburg PA
CBHW021133080526
44587CB00012B/1272